MW00892469

CHOOSING TO BE A MEDIUM

COMPANION JOURNAL

A workbook to accompany *Choosing to be a Medium:*
Experience & Share the Healing Wonder of Spirit Communication by Sharon Farber

Sharon Farber

Book design by Dungeness Communications, Inc.
Cover image by iStockphoto.com 655839766/Free Spirit
Cover design by Dungeness Communications, Inc.
Chapter images artwork by Sharon Farber
Back cover image: Dragonfly on Purple by Sharon Farber
Head shot photo: Craig Norton Photography

ISBN: 9781791901127

Published 2019 by Dragonfly Healing Arts LLC.
www.dragonflyhealingarts.net

Other books by Sharon Farber
Choosing to be a Medium: Experience & Share the Healing Wonder of Spirit Communication (Llewellyn, 2019)
(Blackstone Audio, 2019)

ACKNOWLEDGEMENTS

I'm tremendously grateful to Noelle Tkacz for working with words with me, and Hall Stuart-Lovell for an amazing job on layout, design, and cover.

DISCLAIMER

Not everybody has the ideal emotional strength and stability to be a medium. Good mental health, including a strong connection to reality, is vital. People with certain types of mental illness, including clinical depression or psychosis, are advised to consult a healthcare provider or spiritual mentor before pursing mediumship development.

Do not engage in mediumship when you're feeling physically, mentally, emotionally, or spiritually unhealthy. Do not practice mediumship while depressed, drained, seriously sleep-deprived, or emotionally unstable, nor while drunk or under the influence of mind-altering drugs.

Expressing belief in a supportive and healing afterlife is not to be misconstrued as in any way advocating suicide. Suicide is not a solution to life's problems. If you or someone you know is considering suicide, please call the National Suicide Prevention Lifeline at 1-800-273-8255 in the United States. Outside of the United States, contact the International Association for Suicide Prevention (IASP) at https://www.iasp.info/resources/Crisis_Centres/.

The author does not take any responsibility for any possible consequences that may result from the reader's use of content contained in this publication and recommends common sense when contemplating the practices described in the work.

INTRODUCTION

When my mediumship development began, I was largely on my own. My quest for teachers and appropriate classes was often less than fruitful. I received instruction from several excellent mediums while taking their classes, but I had no mentor to guide me and support my individual needs. I had to create my own course of study, which I based on my experience in massage school decades earlier. An important part of that process was giving practice massages and keeping a log that included results and feedback. I used the same procedure for my mediumship development. Along with taking classes, sitting in circle, and studying everything mediumship, I gave many free readings and wrote up the results. I also sporadically attempted to track my meditations, encounters with guides, and other related material. My notes from these activities were written on scattered papers and typed in obscure locations on my computer. It was not a pretty system.

I wrote *Choosing to be a Medium: Experience & Share the Healing Wonder of Spirit Communication* to offer the type of guidance I wish I had received during my development. The book will empower and transform you as you seek to become a medium. *Choosing to be a Medium Companion Journal* provides additional encouragement to help you maintain focus and grow. The journal creates a single, tangible location to record your readings, meditations, and thoughts—all of which will help you process results and reflect on your progress.

Your mediumistic journey will include spiritual fulfillment and growth. It's all ahead of you! In this journey, strive for inner peace, harmony, and balance. Know that those in spirit love and support you.

Love and light,

Sharon Farber

CONTENTS

Part I: Journal Entries

Use this portion of the book as a sacred space to embrace your mediumistic development without fear of judgement. Answer the prompts honestly and explore your feelings. Record what does and doesn't work; often you learn more from challenges than successes. Work with the prompts as you read the corresponding chapters in *Choosing to be a Medium* or when a theme becomes relevant to your development. Return often to review your progress and update your responses as your awareness shifts.

My Spiritual Journey

Why I want to be a medium: _____
_____
_____
_____
_____

How I know I'm a medium: _____
_____
_____
_____

How long I've known I'm a medium: _____
_____
_____
_____

How comfortable I am with mediumship: _____
_____
_____
_____
_____

How mediumship has changed or will change my life: _____
_____
_____
_____
_____

My previous psychic experiences: _____
_____
_____
_____
_____

My current psychic skills: _____

_____

_____

_____

_____

My previous connections with spirit people (if any): _____

_____

_____

_____

_____

My current mediumistic abilities (if any): _____

_____

_____

_____

_____

I am most intuitive when: _____

_____

_____

_____

What heightens my intuition: _____

_____

_____

_____

Steps I will take to improve my intuition: _____

_____

_____

_____

Methods of raising my vibration I've tried: _____

_____

_____

_____

Results of Exercises 1 – 10 in *Choosing to be a Medium*: _____

_____

_____

_____

_____

_____

_____

_____

_____

_____

_____

_____

_____

_____

_____

_____

_____

_____

_____

_____

_____

_____

_____

_____

_____

_____

_____

_____

_____

_____

_____

_____

Additional Notes: _____

Spirit Guides

What I believe about spirit guides: _____

_____

_____

_____

What I know about my own spirit guides (if anything): _____

_____

_____

_____

Times I've felt guided: _____

_____

_____

_____

Results from following guidance: _____

_____

_____

_____

Results from not following guidance: _____

_____

_____

_____

When I'm most aware of guidance: _____

_____

_____

_____

How I'll become more aware of my guides: _____

_____

_____

_____

Results of Exercise 13: Connect with a Spirit Guide Meditation in *Choosing to be a Medium*: _____

_____

_____

_____

_____

_____

_____

_____

_____

_____

_____

_____

_____

Additional Notes: _____

_____

_____

_____

_____

_____

_____

_____

_____

_____

_____

_____

_____

_____

_____

_____

Addressing My Fear

My fears about mediumship: _____

_____

_____

_____

Why I'm not afraid of spirits: _____

_____

_____

_____

Why I am afraid of spirits: _____

_____

_____

_____

My concerns (if any) about being alienated: _____

_____

_____

_____

My feelings about not being good enough (as a medium): _____

_____

_____

_____

Which fears are scariest and why: _____

_____

_____

_____

Worst-case scenarios: _____

_____

_____

_____

How I'm currently resolving my fears: _____

_____

_____

_____

Affirmations to release my fears: _____

_____

_____

_____

Whom I can ask for help: _____

_____

_____

_____

Further steps I'll take to resolve my fears: _____

_____

_____

_____

Additional Notes: _____

_____

_____

_____

_____

_____

_____

_____

_____

_____

_____

_____

_____

_____

Teachers & Other Resources

Spiritualist churches and centers near me: _____

_____

_____

_____

Classes or workshops available: _____

_____

_____

_____

Teachers and mentors available: _____

_____

_____

_____

Circles near me: _____

_____

_____

_____

Online offerings: _____

_____

_____

_____

Other resources: _____

_____

_____

_____

What kind of teacher(s) I want: _____

_____

_____

_____

What type of circle I'd like to join: _____

_____

_____

_____

My action plan to find the right teachers, classes, and circles: _____

_____

_____

_____

Like-minded people who might want to learn with me: _____

_____

_____

_____

Additional Notes: _____

_____

_____

_____

_____

_____

_____

_____

_____

_____

_____

_____

_____

_____

_____

_____

Preparation & Ritual

Where I'll practice my mediumship development: _____
_____
_____
_____

What's needed to prepare this location: _____
_____
_____
_____

How I feel in this place: _____
_____
_____
_____

What will make it better: _____
_____
_____
_____

How I'll prepare myself: _____
_____
_____
_____

Rituals I've tried: _____
_____
_____
_____

Which rituals are most effective: _____
_____
_____
_____

My favorite rituals: _____

_____

_____

_____

New rituals I'll try: _____

_____

_____

_____

Additional Notes: _____

_____

_____

_____

_____

_____

_____

_____

_____

_____

_____

_____

_____

_____

_____

_____

_____

_____

_____

_____

_____

_____

Grounding & "Raising My Vibration"

How I feel when I'm grounded: _____

_____

_____

_____

How I feel when I'm not grounded: _____

_____

_____

_____

What prevents me from being grounded: _____

_____

_____

_____

What grounds me without even trying: _____

_____

_____

_____

Grounding methods I've tried: _____

_____

_____

_____

What works best: _____

_____

_____

_____

What works when I'm feeling particularly ungrounded: _____

_____

_____

_____

Ways I'll ground myself in preparation for mediumship: _____

_____

_____

_____

Daily practices I'll do to stay grounded: _____

_____

_____

_____

How I feel when my vibration is high: _____

_____

_____

_____

How I feel when my vibration is low: _____

_____

_____

_____

What lowers my vibration: _____

_____

_____

_____

What raises my vibration when I'm not even trying: _____

_____

_____

_____

Methods of raising my vibration I've tried: _____

_____

_____

_____

What works best: _____

_____

_____

_____

Ways I'll raise my vibration in preparation for mediumship: _____

_____

_____

_____

Daily practices I'll do to raise my vibration: _____

_____

_____

_____

_____

Additional Notes: _____

_____

_____

_____

_____

_____

_____

_____

_____

_____

_____

_____

_____

_____

_____

_____

_____

_____

_____

 Setting My Intention

Use your own words for the following situations. Suggestions are found in Chapter 6 of *Choosing to be a Medium.*

Setting my intention to give a private reading: _____

Setting my intention to read for (or within) a group: _____

Setting my intention to end a session: _____

Further thoughts and actions to turn off spirit communication (as needed): _____

_____

_____

_____

_____

_____

_____

_____

_____

_____

Additional Notes: _____

_____

_____

_____

_____

_____

_____

_____

_____

_____

_____

_____

_____

_____

_____

_____

_____

 *Perceiving Spirit People*

Psychic senses I use to perceive spirit people: _____

_____

_____

My strongest psychic senses: _____

_____

_____

Psychic senses I'd like to strengthen: _____

_____

_____

Psychic senses I've not yet experienced: _____

_____

_____

Psychic senses I'd like to experience _____

_____

_____

My plan to develop these psychic senses: _____

_____

_____

_____

_____

My experiences with clairvoyance: _____

_____

_____

_____

_____

_____

My experiences with clairaudience: _____

_____

_____

_____

_____

_____

My experiences with clairsentience: _____

_____

_____

_____

_____

_____

My experiences with claircognizance: _____

_____

_____

_____

_____

My experiences with clairaroma: _____

_____

_____

_____

_____

My experiences with clairgustance: _____

_____

_____

_____

_____

Results of Exercises 30 – 37 in *Choosing to be a Medium*: _____

Additional Notes: _____

_____

_____

_____

_____

_____

_____

_____

_____

_____

_____

_____

_____

_____

_____

_____

_____

_____

_____

_____

_____

_____

_____

_____

_____

_____

_____

_____

_____

_____

_____

_____

SECTION 9

Symbols

Common symbols I use in my everyday life:

Symbol: _____ Meaning: _____

Symbol: _____ Meaning: _____

Symbol: _____ Meaning: _____

Symbol: _____ Meaning: _____

Symbol: _____ Meaning: _____

Symbol: _____ Meaning: _____

Symbol: _____ Meaning: _____

Symbol: _____ Meaning: _____

Symbol: _____ Meaning: _____

Symbol: _____ Meaning: _____

Symbol: _____ Meaning: _____

Symbol: _____ Meaning: _____

Symbol: _____ Meaning: _____

Symbol: _____ Meaning: _____

Symbol: _____ Meaning: _____

Symbol: _____ Meaning: _____

Symbol: _____ Meaning: _____

Symbol: _____ Meaning: _____

Symbol: _____ Meaning: _____

Symbol: _____ Meaning: _____

Symbol: _____ Meaning: _____

Symbol: _____ Meaning: _____

Symbol: _____ Meaning: _____

Symbol: _____ Meaning: _____

Symbol: _____ Meaning: _____

Symbol: _____ Meaning: _____

Symbol: _____ Meaning: _____

Symbols I've experienced in mediumship:

Symbol: _____ Meaning: _____

Symbol: _____ Meaning: _____

Symbol: _____ Meaning: _____

Symbol: _____ Meaning: _____

Symbol: _____ Meaning: _____

Symbol: _____ Meaning: _____

Symbol: _____ Meaning: _____

Symbol: _____ Meaning: _____

Symbol: _____ Meaning: _____

Symbol: _____ Meaning: _____

Symbol: _____ Meaning: _____

Symbol: _____ Meaning: _____

Symbol: _____ Meaning: _____

Symbol: _____ Meaning: _____

Symbol: _____ Meaning: _____

Symbol: _____ Meaning: _____

Symbol: _____ Meaning: _____

Symbol: _____ Meaning: _____

Symbol: _____ Meaning: _____

Symbol: _____ Meaning: _____

Symbol: _____ Meaning: _____

Symbol: _____ Meaning: _____

Symbol: _____ Meaning: _____

Symbol: _____ Meaning: _____

Symbol: _____ Meaning: _____

Symbol: _____ Meaning: _____

Symbol: _____ Meaning: _____

Symbol: _____ Meaning: _____

Symbol: _____ Meaning: _____

Symbol: _____ Meaning: _____

Symbols I'd like spirits to use while communicating with me:

Symbol: _____ Meaning: _____

Symbol: _____ Meaning: _____

Symbol: _____ Meaning: _____

Symbol: _____ Meaning: _____

Symbol: _____ Meaning: _____

Symbol: _____ Meaning: _____

Symbol: _____ Meaning: _____

Symbol: _____ Meaning: _____

Symbol: _____ Meaning: _____

Symbol: _____ Meaning: _____

Symbol: _____ Meaning: _____

Symbol: _____ Meaning: _____

Symbol: _____ Meaning: _____

Symbol: _____ Meaning: _____

Symbol: _____ Meaning: _____

Symbol: _____ Meaning: _____

Symbol: _____ Meaning: _____

Symbol: _____ Meaning: _____

Symbol: _____ Meaning: _____

Symbol: _____ Meaning: _____

Symbol: _____ Meaning: _____

Symbol: _____ Meaning: _____

Symbol: _____ Meaning: _____

Symbol: _____ Meaning: _____

Symbol: _____ Meaning: _____

Symbol: _____ Meaning: _____

Symbol: _____ Meaning: _____

Symbol: _____ Meaning: _____

Symbol: _____ Meaning: _____

Symbol: _____ Meaning: _____

Symbol: _____ Meaning: _____

Symbol: _____ Meaning: _____

Symbol: _____ Meaning: _____

SECTION 10

Boundaries & Self-Care

How I keep good boundaries in my physical life: _____

_____

_____

How I keep good boundaries in my spiritual life: _____

_____

_____

_____

Where I need to improve my boundaries: _____

_____

_____

_____

How I'll improve my boundaries: _____

_____

_____

_____

How I close myself to spirit communication: _____

_____

_____

_____

What I do if I want a spirit person to leave: _____

_____

_____

_____

What I do if a spirit person is too close: _____

_____

_____

_____

Spirit people (if any) who are always welcome: _____

_____

_____

_____

Ways I take care of myself: _____

_____

_____

_____

_____

Ways I don't take care of myself: _____

_____

_____

_____

_____

Habits that strengthen me: _____

_____

_____

_____

_____

Habits that weaken me: _____

_____

_____

_____

_____

Changes I will make for my highest good: _____

_____

_____

_____

_____

_____

Additional Notes: _____

_____

_____

_____

_____

_____

_____

_____

_____

_____

_____

_____

_____

_____

_____

_____

_____

_____

_____

_____

_____

_____

_____

_____

_____

_____

_____

_____

_____

_____

_____

_____

Coming Out

How comfortable I am with being known as a medium: _____

_____

_____

_____

I want the following people to know I'm a medium: _____

_____

_____

_____

Whom (if anyone) I don't want to know I'm a medium: _____

_____

_____

_____

What I'll do if these people find out I'm a medium: _____

_____

_____

_____

Worst-case scenarios and how I'll deal with them: _____

_____

_____

_____

I can count on the following people to support my spiritual development: _____

_____

_____

_____

Ways I'll find additional support for my spiritual journey: _____

_____

_____

_____

Additional Notes: _____

_____

_____

_____

_____

_____

_____

_____

_____

_____

_____

_____

_____

_____

_____

_____

_____

_____

_____

_____

_____

_____

_____

_____

_____

_____

_____

_____

_____

_____

_____

_____

Goals

What type(s) of mediumship I want to do: _____
_____
_____
_____

What tools (if any) I want to use: _____
_____
_____
_____

Where I want to do mediumship: _____
_____
_____
_____

Whom I want to do mediumship for: _____
_____
_____
_____

Whom (if anyone) I want to do mediumship with: _____
_____
_____
_____

How far I want to take my mediumship: _____
_____
_____
_____

Steps I will take to accomplish my goals: _____
_____
_____
_____

Additional Notes: _____

_____

_____

_____

_____

_____

_____

_____

_____

_____

_____

_____

_____

_____

_____

_____

_____

_____

_____

_____

_____

_____

_____

_____

_____

_____

_____

_____

_____

_____

_____

_____

_____

Part II: Logs

Use these pages to document your efforts and experiences in spiritual development. Maintaining a record will keep you accountable and encourage commitment. Read the corresponding sections in Chapter 5 of *Choosing to be a Medium* to help you complete the first three logs.

The Reading Log is a particularly important tool to validate your mediumistic abilities. Reading through past entries will be exceptionally valuable if you lack confidence, or experience moments of doubt about your ability to connect with spirit. I often must repeatedly remind students of their successful connections when they're questioning themselves. Your own notes will reinforce the awareness that you are communicating with those on the other side, and no, it isn't your imagination.

Meditation

Type of meditation: silent, moving, flame, mantra, guided, other
Results: challenging, relaxing, distracted, peaceful, sleepy, helpful, insightful, other

1. Date: _____ Type: _____ Length: _____

Results: _____

_____

_____

2. Date: _____ Type: _____ Length: _____

Results: _____

_____

_____

3. Date: _____ Type: _____ Length: _____

Results: _____

_____

_____

4. Date: _____ Type: _____ Length: _____

Results: _____

_____

_____

5. Date: _____ Type: _____ Length: _____

Results: _____

_____

_____

6. Date: _____ Type: _____ Length: _____

Results: _____

_____

_____

_____

7. Date: _____ Type: _____ Length: _____

Results: _____

_____

_____

_____

8. Date: _____ Type: _____ Length: _____

Results: _____

_____

_____

_____

9. Date: _____ Type: _____ Length: _____

Results: _____

_____

_____

_____

10. Date: _____ Type: _____ Length: _____

Results: _____

_____

_____

_____

11. Date: _____ Type: _____ Length: _____

Results: _____

_____

_____

_____

_____

12. Date: _____ Type: _____ Length: _____

Results: _____

_____

_____

_____

13. Date: _____ Type: _____ Length: _____

Results: _____

_____

_____

_____

14. Date: _____ Type: _____ Length: _____

Results: _____

_____

_____

_____

15. Date: _____ Type: _____ Length: _____

Results: _____

_____

_____

_____

16. Date: _____ Type: _____ Length: _____

Results: _____

_____

_____

_____

17. Date: _____ Type: _____ Length: _____

Results: _____

_____

_____

_____

18. Date: _____ Type: _____ Length: _____

Results: _____

_____

_____

_____

19. Date: _____ Type: _____ Length: _____

Results: _____

_____

_____

_____

20. Date: _____ Type: _____ Length: _____

Results: _____

_____

_____

Additional Notes: _____

_____

_____

_____

_____

_____

_____

_____

_____

_____

_____

_____

_____

_____

Breathwork

Type of breathwork: simple breathing, alternate nostril, breath counting, other
Results: challenging, relaxing, distracted, peaceful, empowering, insightful, other

1. Date: _____ Type: _____ Length: _____

Results: _____

_____

_____

_____

2. Date: _____ Type: _____ Length: _____

Results: _____

_____

_____

_____

3. Date: _____ Type: _____ Length: _____

Results: _____

_____

_____

_____

4. Date: _____ Type: _____ Length: _____

Results: _____

_____

_____

_____

5. Date: _____ Type: _____ Length: _____

Results: _____

_____

_____

_____

6. Date: _____ Type: _____ Length: _____

Results: _____

_____

_____

_____

7. Date: _____ Type: _____ Length: _____

Results: _____

_____

_____

_____

8. Date: _____ Type: _____ Length: _____

Results: _____

_____

_____

_____

9. Date: _____ Type: _____ Length: _____

Results: _____

_____

_____

_____

10. Date: _____ Type: _____ Length: _____

Results: _____

_____

_____

_____

11. Date: _____ Type: _____ Length: _____

Results: _____

_____

_____

_____

12. Date: _____ Type: _____ Length: _____
Results: _____
_____
_____
_____

13. Date: _____ Type: _____ Length: _____
Results: _____
_____
_____
_____

14. Date: _____ Type: _____ Length: _____
Results: _____
_____
_____
_____

15. Date: _____ Type: _____ Length: _____
Results: _____
_____
_____
_____

16. Date: _____ Type: _____ Length: _____
Results: _____
_____
_____
_____

17. Date: _____ Type: _____ Length: _____
Results: _____
_____
_____
_____

18. Date: _____ Type: _____ Length: _____

Results: _____

_____

_____

_____

19. Date: _____ Type: _____ Length: _____

Results: _____

_____

_____

_____

20. Date: _____ Type: _____ Length: _____

Results: _____

_____

_____

Additional Notes: _____

_____

_____

_____

_____

_____

_____

_____

_____

_____

_____

_____

_____

_____

Sitting in the Power

Type of sitting in the power: live guidance, recorded guidance, on my own, other
Results: challenging, distracted, peaceful, sleepy, powerful, amazing, insightful, other

1. Date: _____ Type: _____ Length: _____

Results: _____

_____

_____

2. Date: _____ Type: _____ Length: _____

Results: _____

_____

_____

3. Date: _____ Type: _____ Length: _____

Results: _____

_____

_____

4. Date: _____ Type: _____ Length: _____

Results: _____

_____

_____

5. Date: _____ Type: _____ Length: _____

Results: _____

_____

_____

6. Date: _____ Type: _____ Length: _____

Results: _____

_____

_____

_____

7. Date: _____ Type: _____ Length: _____

Results: _____

_____

_____

_____

8. Date: _____ Type: _____ Length: _____

Results: _____

_____

_____

_____

9. Date: _____ Type: _____ Length: _____

Results: _____

_____

_____

_____

10. Date: _____ Type: _____ Length: _____

Results: _____

_____

_____

_____

11. Date: _____ Type: _____ Length: _____

Results: _____

_____

_____

_____

12. Date: _____ Type: _____ Length: _____

Results: _____

_____

_____

_____

13. Date: _____ Type: _____ Length: _____

Results: _____

_____

_____

_____

14. Date: _____ Type: _____ Length: _____

Results: _____

_____

_____

_____

15. Date: _____ Type: _____ Length: _____

Results: _____

_____

_____

_____

16. Date: _____ Type: _____ Length: _____

Results: _____

_____

_____

_____

17. Date: _____ Type: _____ Length: _____

Results: _____

_____

_____

_____

18. Date: _____ Type: _____ Length: _____

Results: _____

_____

_____

_____

19. Date: _____ Type: _____ Length: _____

Results: _____

_____

_____

_____

20. Date: _____ Type: _____ Length: _____

Results: _____

_____

_____

_____

Additional Notes: _____

_____

_____

_____

_____

_____

_____

_____

_____

_____

_____

_____

_____

_____

_____

Readings

Type of reading: in person, phone, video, remote, other
Location: home, office, church, fair, outside, other
Relationship to sitter(s): friend, family, acquaintance, stranger, other

1. Date: _____ Type: _____ Length: _____

Location: _____ Sitter(s): _____

Relationship to sitter(s): _____

What spirit people came through: _____

What evidence was provided: _____

What messages (if any): _____

What was validated by the sitter(s): _____

My feelings about this reading: _____

What would have improved the session: _____

2. Date: _____ Type: _____ Length: _____

Location: _____ Sitter(s): _____

Relationship to sitter(s): _____

What spirit people came through: _____

_____

What evidence was provided: _____

_____

What messages (if any): _____

_____

What was validated by the sitter(s): _____

_____

My feelings about this reading: _____

_____

What would have improved the session: _____

_____

3. Date: _____ Type: _____ Length: _____

Location: _____ Sitter(s): _____

Relationship to sitter(s): _____

What spirit people came through: _____

_____

What evidence was provided: _____

_____

What messages (if any): _____

_____

What was validated by the sitter(s): _____

_____

My feelings about this reading: _____

_____

What would have improved the session: _____

_____

4. Date: _____ Type: _____ Length: _____

Location: _____ Sitter(s): _____

Relationship to sitter(s): _____

What spirit people came through: _____

_____

What evidence was provided: _____

_____

What messages (if any): _____

_____

What was validated by the sitter(s): _____

_____

My feelings about this reading: _____

_____

What would have improved the session: _____

_____

5. Date: _____ Type: _____ Length: _____

Location: _____ Sitter(s): _____

Relationship to sitter(s): _____

What spirit people came through: _____

_____

What evidence was provided: _____

_____

What messages (if any): _____

_____

What was validated by the sitter(s): _____

_____

My feelings about this reading: _____

_____

What would have improved the session: _____

_____

6. Date: _____ Type: _____ Length: _____

Location: _____ Sitter(s): _____

Relationship to sitter(s): _____

What spirit people came through: _____

_____

What evidence was provided: _____

_____

What messages (if any): _____

_____

What was validated by the sitter(s): _____

_____

My feelings about this reading: _____

_____

What would have improved the session: _____

_____

7. Date: _____ Type: _____ Length: _____

Location: _____ Sitter(s): _____

Relationship to sitter(s): _____

What spirit people came through: _____

_____

What evidence was provided: _____

_____

What messages (if any): _____

_____

What was validated by the sitter(s): _____

_____

My feelings about this reading: _____

_____

What would have improved the session: _____

_____

8. Date: _____ Type: _____ Length: _____

Location: _____ Sitter(s): _____

Relationship to sitter(s): _____

What spirit people came through: _____

_____

What evidence was provided: _____

_____

What messages (if any): _____

_____

What was validated by the sitter(s): _____

_____

My feelings about this reading: _____

_____

What would have improved the session: _____

_____

9. Date: _____ Type: _____ Length: _____

Location: _____ Sitter(s): _____

Relationship to sitter(s): _____

What spirit people came through: _____

_____

What evidence was provided: _____

_____

What messages (if any): _____

_____

What was validated by the sitter(s): _____

_____

My feelings about this reading: _____

_____

What would have improved the session: _____

_____

10. Date: _____ Type: _____ Length: _____

Location: _____ Sitter(s): _____

Relationship to sitter(s): _____

What spirit people came through: _____

_____

What evidence was provided: _____

_____

What messages (if any): _____

_____

What was validated by the sitter(s): _____

_____

My feelings about this reading: _____

_____

What would have improved the session: _____

_____

11. Date: _____ Type: _____ Length: _____

Location: _____ Sitter(s): _____

Relationship to sitter(s): _____

What spirit people came through: _____

_____

What evidence was provided: _____

_____

What messages (if any): _____

_____

What was validated by the sitter(s): _____

_____

My feelings about this reading: _____

_____

What would have improved the session: _____

_____

12. Date: _____ Type: _____ Length: _____

Location: _____ Sitter(s): _____

Relationship to sitter(s): _____

What spirit people came through: _____

_____

What evidence was provided: _____

_____

What messages (if any): _____

_____

What was validated by the sitter(s): _____

_____

My feelings about this reading: _____

_____

What would have improved the session: _____

_____

13. Date: _____ Type: _____ Length: _____

Location: _____ Sitter(s): _____

Relationship to sitter(s): _____

What spirit people came through: _____

_____

What evidence was provided: _____

_____

What messages (if any): _____

_____

What was validated by the sitter(s): _____

_____

My feelings about this reading: _____

_____

What would have improved the session: _____

_____

14. Date: _____ Type: _____ Length: _____

Location: _____ Sitter(s): _____

Relationship to sitter(s): _____

What spirit people came through: _____

_____

What evidence was provided: _____

_____

What messages (if any): _____

_____

What was validated by the sitter(s): _____

_____

My feelings about this reading: _____

_____

What would have improved the session: _____

_____

15. Date: _____ Type: _____ Length: _____

Location: _____ Sitter(s): _____

Relationship to sitter(s): _____

What spirit people came through: _____

_____

What evidence was provided: _____

_____

What messages (if any): _____

_____

What was validated by the sitter(s): _____

_____

My feelings about this reading: _____

_____

What would have improved the session: _____

_____

16. Date: _____ Type: _____ Length: _____

Location: _____ Sitter(s): _____

Relationship to sitter(s): _____

What spirit people came through: _____

_____

What evidence was provided: _____

_____

What messages (if any): _____

_____

What was validated by the sitter(s): _____

_____

My feelings about this reading: _____

_____

What would have improved the session: _____

_____

17. Date: _____ Type: _____ Length: _____

Location: _____ Sitter(s): _____

Relationship to sitter(s): _____

What spirit people came through: _____

_____

What evidence was provided: _____

_____

What messages (if any): _____

_____

What was validated by the sitter(s): _____

_____

My feelings about this reading: _____

_____

What would have improved the session: _____

_____

18. Date: _____ Type: _____ Length: _____

Location: _____ Sitter(s): _____

Relationship to sitter(s): _____

What spirit people came through: _____

_____

What evidence was provided: _____

_____

What messages (if any): _____

_____

What was validated by the sitter(s): _____

_____

My feelings about this reading: _____

_____

What would have improved the session: _____

_____

19. Date: _____ Type: _____ Length: _____

Location: _____ Sitter(s): _____

Relationship to sitter(s): _____

What spirit people came through: _____

_____

What evidence was provided: _____

_____

What messages (if any): _____

_____

What was validated by the sitter(s): _____

_____

My feelings about this reading: _____

_____

What would have improved the session: _____

_____

20. Date: _____ Type: _____ Length: _____

Location: _____ Sitter(s): _____

Relationship to sitter(s): _____

What spirit people came through: _____

_____

What evidence was provided: _____

_____

What messages (if any): _____

_____

What was validated by the sitter(s): _____

_____

My feelings about this reading: _____

_____

What would have improved the session: _____

_____

21. Date: _____ Type: _____ Length: _____

Location: _____ Sitter(s): _____

Relationship to sitter(s): _____

What spirit people came through: _____

_____

What evidence was provided: _____

_____

What messages (if any): _____

_____

What was validated by the sitter(s): _____

_____

My feelings about this reading: _____

_____

What would have improved the session: _____

_____

22. Date: _____ Type: _____ Length: _____

Location: _____ Sitter(s): _____

Relationship to sitter(s): _____

What spirit people came through: _____

_____

What evidence was provided: _____

_____

What messages (if any): _____

_____

What was validated by the sitter(s): _____

_____

My feelings about this reading: _____

_____

What would have improved the session: _____

_____

23. Date: _____ Type: _____ Length: _____

Location: _____ Sitter(s): _____

Relationship to sitter(s): _____

What spirit people came through: _____

_____

What evidence was provided: _____

_____

What messages (if any): _____

_____

What was validated by the sitter(s): _____

_____

My feelings about this reading: _____

_____

What would have improved the session: _____

_____

24. Date: _____ Type: _____ Length: _____

Location: _____ Sitter(s): _____

Relationship to sitter(s): _____

What spirit people came through: _____

_____

What evidence was provided: _____

_____

What messages (if any): _____

_____

What was validated by the sitter(s): _____

_____

My feelings about this reading: _____

_____

What would have improved the session: _____

_____

25. Date: _____ Type: _____ Length: _____

Location: _____ Sitter(s): _____

Relationship to sitter(s): _____

What spirit people came through: _____

_____

What evidence was provided: _____

_____

What messages (if any): _____

_____

What was validated by the sitter(s): _____

_____

My feelings about this reading: _____

_____

What would have improved the session: _____

_____

26. Date: _____ Type: _____ Length: _____

Location: _____ Sitter(s): _____

Relationship to sitter(s): _____

What spirit people came through: _____

_____

What evidence was provided: _____

_____

What messages (if any): _____

_____

What was validated by the sitter(s): _____

_____

My feelings about this reading: _____

_____

What would have improved the session: _____

_____

27. Date: _____ Type: _____ Length: _____

Location: _____ Sitter(s): _____

Relationship to sitter(s): _____

What spirit people came through: _____

_____

What evidence was provided: _____

_____

What messages (if any): _____

_____

What was validated by the sitter(s): _____

_____

My feelings about this reading: _____

_____

What would have improved the session: _____

_____

28. Date: _____ Type: _____ Length: _____

Location: _____ Sitter(s): _____

Relationship to sitter(s): _____

What spirit people came through: _____

_____

What evidence was provided: _____

_____

What messages (if any): _____

_____

What was validated by the sitter(s): _____

_____

My feelings about this reading: _____

_____

What would have improved the session: _____

_____

29. Date: _____ Type: _____ Length: _____

Location: _____ Sitter(s): _____

Relationship to sitter(s): _____

What spirit people came through: _____

_____

What evidence was provided: _____

_____

What messages (if any): _____

_____

What was validated by the sitter(s): _____

_____

My feelings about this reading: _____

_____

What would have improved the session: _____

_____

30. Date: _____ Type: _____ Length: _____

Location: _____ Sitter(s): _____

Relationship to sitter(s): _____

What spirit people came through: _____

_____

What evidence was provided: _____

_____

What messages (if any): _____

_____

What was validated by the sitter(s): _____

_____

My feelings about this reading: _____

_____

What would have improved the session: _____

_____

31. Date: _____ Type: _____ Length: _____

Location: _____ Sitter(s): _____

Relationship to sitter(s): _____

What spirit people came through: _____

_____

What evidence was provided: _____

_____

What messages (if any): _____

_____

What was validated by the sitter(s): _____

_____

My feelings about this reading: _____

_____

What would have improved the session: _____

_____

32. Date: _____ Type: _____ Length: _____

Location: _____ Sitter(s): _____

Relationship to sitter(s): _____

What spirit people came through: _____

_____

What evidence was provided: _____

_____

What messages (if any): _____

_____

What was validated by the sitter(s): _____

_____

My feelings about this reading: _____

_____

What would have improved the session: _____

_____

33. Date: _____ Type: _____ Length: _____

Location: _____ Sitter(s): _____

Relationship to sitter(s): _____

What spirit people came through: _____

_____

What evidence was provided: _____

_____

What messages (if any): _____

_____

What was validated by the sitter(s): _____

_____

My feelings about this reading: _____

_____

What would have improved the session: _____

_____

34. Date: _____ Type: _____ Length: _____

Location: _____ Sitter(s): _____

Relationship to sitter(s): _____

What spirit people came through: _____

_____

What evidence was provided: _____

_____

What messages (if any): _____

_____

What was validated by the sitter(s): _____

_____

My feelings about this reading: _____

_____

What would have improved the session: _____

_____

35. Date: _____ Type: _____ Length: _____

Location: _____ Sitter(s): _____

Relationship to sitter(s): _____

What spirit people came through: _____

_____

What evidence was provided: _____

_____

What messages (if any): _____

_____

What was validated by the sitter(s): _____

_____

My feelings about this reading: _____

_____

What would have improved the session: _____

_____

36. Date: _____ Type: _____ Length: _____

Location: _____ Sitter(s): _____

Relationship to sitter(s): _____

What spirit people came through: _____

_____

What evidence was provided: _____

_____

What messages (if any): _____

_____

What was validated by the sitter(s): _____

_____

My feelings about this reading: _____

_____

What would have improved the session: _____

_____

37. Date: _____ Type: _____ Length: _____

Location: _____ Sitter(s): _____

Relationship to sitter(s): _____

What spirit people came through: _____

_____

What evidence was provided: _____

_____

What messages (if any): _____

_____

What was validated by the sitter(s): _____

_____

My feelings about this reading: _____

_____

What would have improved the session: _____

_____

38. Date: _____ Type: _____ Length: _____

Location: _____ Sitter(s): _____

Relationship to sitter(s): _____

What spirit people came through: _____

_____

What evidence was provided: _____

_____

What messages (if any): _____

_____

What was validated by the sitter(s): _____

_____

My feelings about this reading: _____

_____

What would have improved the session: _____

_____

39. Date: _____ Type: _____ Length: _____

Location: _____ Sitter(s): _____

Relationship to sitter(s): _____

What spirit people came through: _____

_____

What evidence was provided: _____

_____

What messages (if any): _____

_____

What was validated by the sitter(s): _____

_____

My feelings about this reading: _____

_____

What would have improved the session: _____

_____

40. Date: _____ Type: _____ Length: _____

Location: _____ Sitter(s): _____

Relationship to sitter(s): _____

What spirit people came through: _____

_____

What evidence was provided: _____

_____

What messages (if any): _____

_____

What was validated by the sitter(s): _____

_____

My feelings about this reading: _____

_____

What would have improved the session: _____

_____

41. Date: _____ Type: _____ Length: _____

Location: _____ Sitter(s): _____

Relationship to sitter(s): _____

What spirit people came through: _____

_____

What evidence was provided: _____

_____

What messages (if any): _____

_____

What was validated by the sitter(s): _____

_____

My feelings about this reading: _____

_____

What would have improved the session: _____

_____

42. Date: _____ Type: _____ Length: _____

Location: _____ Sitter(s): _____

Relationship to sitter(s): _____

What spirit people came through: _____

_____

What evidence was provided: _____

_____

What messages (if any): _____

_____

What was validated by the sitter(s): _____

_____

My feelings about this reading: _____

_____

What would have improved the session: _____

_____

43. Date: _____ Type: _____ Length: _____

Location: _____ Sitter(s): _____

Relationship to sitter(s): _____

What spirit people came through: _____

_____

What evidence was provided: _____

_____

What messages (if any): _____

_____

What was validated by the sitter(s): _____

_____

My feelings about this reading: _____

_____

What would have improved the session: _____

_____

44. Date: _____ Type: _____ Length: _____

Location: _____ Sitter(s): _____

Relationship to sitter(s): _____

What spirit people came through: _____

_____

What evidence was provided: _____

_____

What messages (if any): _____

_____

What was validated by the sitter(s): _____

_____

My feelings about this reading: _____

_____

What would have improved the session: _____

_____

45. Date: _____ Type: _____ Length: _____

Location: _____ Sitter(s): _____

Relationship to sitter(s): _____

What spirit people came through: _____

_____

What evidence was provided: _____

_____

What messages (if any): _____

_____

What was validated by the sitter(s): _____

_____

My feelings about this reading: _____

_____

What would have improved the session: _____

_____

46. Date: _____ Type: _____ Length: _____

Location: _____ Sitter(s): _____

Relationship to sitter(s): _____

What spirit people came through: _____
_____

What evidence was provided: _____
_____

What messages (if any): _____
_____

What was validated by the sitter(s): _____
_____

My feelings about this reading: _____
_____

What would have improved the session: _____
_____

47. Date: _____ Type: _____ Length: _____

Location: _____ Sitter(s): _____

Relationship to sitter(s): _____

What spirit people came through: _____
_____

What evidence was provided: _____
_____

What messages (if any): _____
_____

What was validated by the sitter(s): _____
_____

My feelings about this reading: _____
_____

What would have improved the session: _____
_____

48. Date: _____ Type: _____ Length: _____

Location: _____ Sitter(s): _____

Relationship to sitter(s): _____

What spirit people came through: _____

_____

What evidence was provided: _____

_____

What messages (if any): _____

_____

What was validated by the sitter(s): _____

_____

My feelings about this reading: _____

_____

What would have improved the session: _____

_____

49. Date: _____ Type: _____ Length: _____

Location: _____ Sitter(s): _____

Relationship to sitter(s): _____

What spirit people came through: _____

_____

What evidence was provided: _____

_____

What messages (if any): _____

_____

What was validated by the sitter(s): _____

_____

My feelings about this reading: _____

_____

What would have improved the session: _____

_____

50. Date: _____ Type: _____ Length: _____

Location: _____ Sitter(s): _____

Relationship to sitter(s): _____

What spirit people came through: _____
_____

What evidence was provided: _____
_____

What messages (if any): _____
_____

What was validated by the sitter(s): _____
_____

My feelings about this reading: _____
_____

What would have improved the session: _____
_____

Additional Notes: _____
_____
_____
_____
_____
_____
_____
_____
_____
_____
_____
_____

Monday July 10th

Joe

Gardener / Gardening
Guide?

Candle Flame
w/ flare on side?

Creepy Crawlies

Grasshopper

Glasses

Nose of Deer

*Holding hands w/ older
Woman SADNESS - Tears, (Relief) contact

Heavy Jewelery, Beads, Necklace?
-chains?

Weep Weep weep Biderwwwwwww
-Robin / Blue Jay?

Wed. July 10th
"Joe" from Abbott ertz
Connection-

Rose-Red, Lilies,
MARYANN
Yellow Bird - Parot or
Parakeet?

SO SORRY!
-so much Love.

??

Made in the USA
Monee, IL
13 August 2022

11533244R10046